JOHN AUDUBON
EXPLORES FLORIDA

POEMS

Thomas Peter Bennett

Goose River Press
Waldoboro, Maine

Library of Congress Card Number: 2023945358

ISBN: 978-1-59713-268-8 Paperback

First Printing, 2023

Published by
Goose River Press
3400 Friendship Road
Waldoboro ME 04572
e-mail: gooseriverpress@gmail.com
www.gooseriverpress.com

A Dream

John James Audubon dreamed
        of exploring Florida, after it had been
popularized by William Bartram's
        Travels, and the natural
history discoveries of others.

Audubon's inspiration was
        to focus on drawings and
describing the birds of Florida
        for his "Great Work" in progress.

Audubon's dream culminated in
        his exploration of Florida
along Bartram's and others'
        tracks—and further
south to Key West—
        seeking new, unique
American birds.

Preface

After the publication of the first volume of *The Birds of America* and its heralded reception in Philadelphia and London, Audubon departed from England in July 1831 for his next adventure: to pursue Florida waterbirds and other regional exotics. Accompanying him on the ship were his wife Lucy and Henry Ward, a young English taxidermist whom Audubon had engaged to assist in collecting and preserving specimens during the Florida expedition. Their first destination was Philadelphia, where Audubon hired George Lehman, a Swiss landscape painter, to accompany him and Ward in Florida. Mrs. Audubon departed for Louisville. Audubon also arranged with G.W. Featherstonehaugh, the editor of *The Monthly American Journal of Geology and Natural Science*, to publish reports of their Florida journey.

Florida at the time was a United States territory. It had been under colonial rule by Spain from the 16th to the 19th century, and briefly by Great Britain during the 18th century. This was followed again by Spain before Florida became a formal territory of the United States in 1821. In 1845, Florida would become the 27th U.S. state.

In late September 1821, Audubon and his two assistants traveled to Washington. Here, the Secretary of the Navy and the Secretary of the Treasury approved the party's travel out of Charleston on a government revenue cutter to the Floridian coastal outposts between St. Augustine and Key West. The party left Washington and traveled by various modes of transport until, in Audubon's words, they "at length approached Charleston . . . with unfeigned delight."

In Charleston, Audubon met and befriended Reverend John Bachman, a friend of ornithologist Alexander Wilson, who also had a passion for birds and roaming the woods. Bachman shared the amenities of his home with Audubon's party during their stay in Charleston while they awaited the arrival of the government cutter for Florida.

Audubon's expedition was intended to last from late November 1831 to the end of May 1832. It included the north Florida area, which had been explored by William Bartram in his *Travels*, and it would continue along the Atlantic coast to Key West. However, circumstances changed, and Audubon's party first explored slightly southward near St. Augustine, then around the St. Johns River, from November 20, 1831, until March 5, 1832. They returned to Charleston and spent a month with Bachman, then traveled directly to the Florida Keys, where they explored from April 15 through May 31, 1832.

For Audubon, as reflected in his letters and journal entries, the north Florida exploration was less productive and less enjoyable than their exploration of the Florida Keys. Both areas prompted his many paintings, writings, and letters about Florida's birds and natural history. ***These inspired and informed John Audubon Explores Florida: Poems***.

Thomas Peter Bennett
Silver Spring , Maryland
3/2/2023

Acknowledgements

Portrait of John James Audubon by John Syme, 1826. Syme's portrait of Audubon, donated to the White House collection in 1962, is an abiding reminder of an American naturalist whose legacy continues to resonate across the ages.

Many thanks to the authors of the books listed under "References" at the end of this book. Special thanks to Deborah Benner, Editor of Goose River Press, and The *Goose River Anthology* where "A Dream" and several other Audubon related poems were published.

Contents

Map of two Audubon trips from Charleston to East Florida and the Keys. (Courtesy of Brad Sanders).

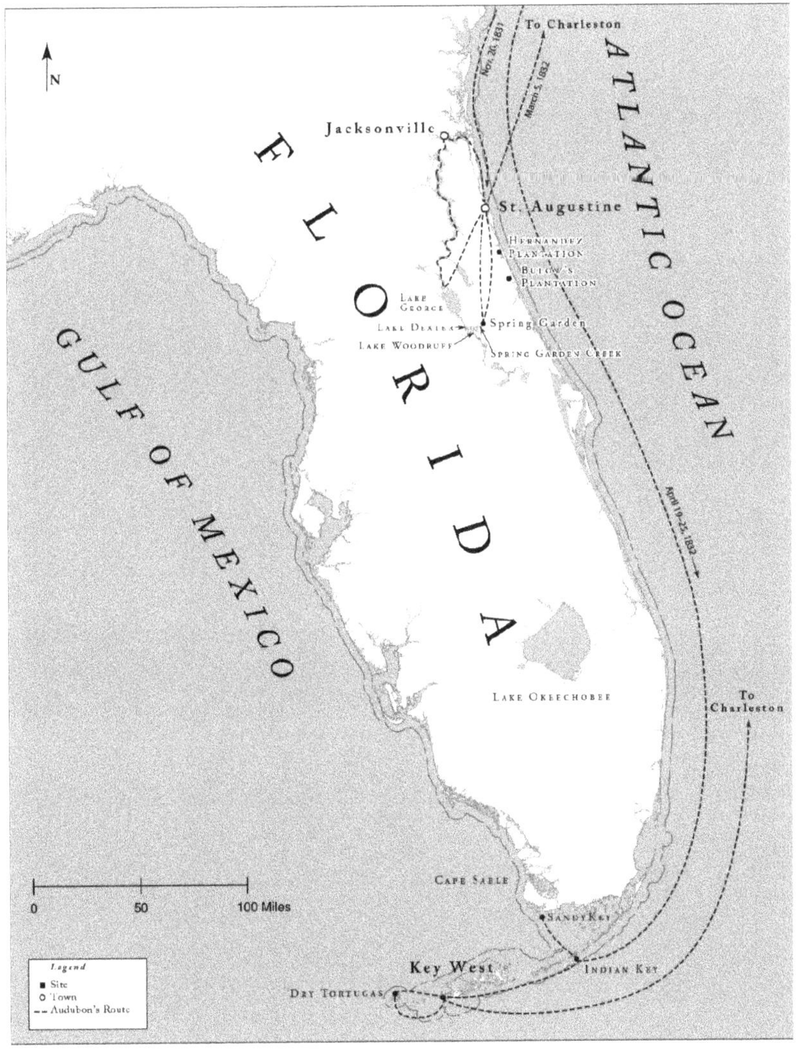

Chronology (Key dates of range)

1831

Philadelphia and Washington to Charleston by steamer and
land transport

Oct. 23	Charleston, at the home of Reverend Bachman
Nov.15	Charleston to St. Augustine on the schooner *Agnes*
Nov. 20	St. Augustine
Dec. 14	Hernandez Plantation, 30 miles south
Dec. 25	Bulow Plantation, 15 miles south
Dec. 28	Overnight trip with Bulow down the Halifax River to Live Oak Landing; returns the following day

1832

Jan. 6	To Spring Garden, Colonel Rees' plantation, southward.
Jan. 14	Returns to St. Augustine
Jan. 25	Sails on schooner *Sparks*, St. Johns River trip; returns because of weather
Feb. 5	Repeats River trip on *Sparks*
Feb. 17	Various stops; bad weather; disembarks and walks to St. Augustine
Mar. 5	Leaves St. Augustine aboard schooner *Agnes* for Charleston
Mar. 15	Arrives in Charleston at the home of Bachman
Apr. 19	Leaves Charleston aboard U.S. Revenue Cutter *Marion* for the Florida Keys
Apr. 24	Views Cape Florida Light (Key Biscayne)
Apr. 25	Anchors at Indian Key, sails through the Keys with many stops; Key West and a trip to Dry Tortugas

<table>
<tr><td>May 10</td><td>Tortugas; boarding of vessels, including wreckers; various islands</td></tr>
<tr><td>May 14</td><td>"Crew principally employed gathering shells etc. for J.J. Audubon"</td></tr>
<tr><td>May 16</td><td>Returns to Key West and the surrounding area</td></tr>
<tr><td>May 21–28</td><td>Sails to Indian Key; visits various keys, Sandy Key, Cape Sable</td></tr>
<tr><td>May 31</td><td>Departs Indian Key and returns to Charleston</td></tr>
</table>

JOHN AUDUBON
EXPLORES FLORIDA

POEMS

1.
To Charleston

The party left Washington and traveled by various modes of transport until they "at length approached Charleston . . . with unfeigned delight," They stayed in Charleston October 23 to November 15, 1831, at the home of Reverend Bachman. Drawing, collecting, and conducting field work.

Charleston

**Figure 1. Long-billed Curlews, Charleston
(Pl. 231)**

Audubon and his assistants
    left Washington and
by steamer and land transport
    "on a dreary journey"
until they approached Charleston, where
    "the view of the city across the bay was
hailed with unfeigned delight."

The next day, Audubon met an ardent admirer,
　　Reverend John Bachman,
who shared Audubon's enthusiasm for
　　birds and wilderness, and was an
"old friend of Alexander Wilson.
　　He shoots well, is an ornithologist,
a philosophical naturalist, and during the time,
we enjoyed his hospitality, he took us all over the
　　country with his carriages and servants in
search of specimens."
　　Audubon and his assistants were
"removed in a jiffy to his own mansion,
　　introduced to the family, and at work the very
next morning."

At Charleston

We are spending another Sunday
        under the hospitable roof of
my most excellent friend,
        the Reverend John Bachmann.
We have been here just three weeks and
        I have drawn fifteen birds, which make
five drawings, all of which are finished by Lehman,
        with views plants &c…
Henry has skinned and preserved 220 specimens
        of 60 different species of birds.

Doctor Sam Wilson gave me an excellent and
        beautiful Newfoundland dog . . .
The papers here have blown me up sky high.
        The Society of Natural Sciences of Philadelphia

has at last elected me one of their members.
        The papers say *Unanimously* . . .

On November 13, Audubon wrote to Lucy,
        "We will leave this hospitable place
on the day after tomorrow at 8 o'clock
        of the morning for St. Augustine, Florida."

2.
Charleston to St. Augustine
November 15–20, 1831

"Having sailed for the Floridas,
     we, after some delay,
occasioned by adverse winds,
     put into a harbor near St. Simons Island,
where I was so fortunate as to meet
     with Thomas Butler King, Esq., who,
after replenishing our provision-stores,
     subscribed to the 'The Birds of America.'
At length we were safely landed at St. Augustine
     and commenced our investigation."

St. Augustine in November

Historian Michael Gannon
     recently commented,
"When the pilgrims arrived in Plymouth, 1620,
     St, Augustine was up for urban renewal!
The first Thanksgiving was
     Celebrated in St. Augustine, 1565!"

Royal Botanist John Bartram
     wrote in 1765,
"November 22 this morning early,
     as well as last night,
thundered at a distance W. N. W.
     About sunrise, the day was showery,
and at a temperature of 67. We set out for Augustine.
     Billy walked and I rode on a hired horse."

Figure 2. Greenshank. St. Augustine
(Pl. 346)

Audubon wrote from St. Augustine,
>East Florida, on 23 November 1831,
"The streets are about ten feet wide and deeply sanded.
>*An old Spanish castle, once the pride of this peninsula*
but now decaying fast.
>*It is built of shell stone . . . curious to the geologist."*

And he notes that nearby,
>*"we went on St. Anastasia's Island and*
collected some hundreds of shells,
>*saw great numbers of water fowls, pelicans, etc.*
Have shot only two birds to draw —
>*One a beautiful heron, the other a sandpiper."*

Caracara Eagle

*"Until my visit to the Floridas
          I was not aware of
The Caracara or Brazilian Eagle
          in the United States.*

*Near St. Augustine, I observed
          a bird flying at a great elevation.
Unknown to me, and bent on obtaining it,
          I followed nearly a mile . . .
and saw it sail for the earth.*

*The bird landed on a dead horse,
          where turkey buzzards and
carrion crow were feeding
          on the savory carcass.*

I crawled along a deep ditch,
          pushing my gun before me,
making occasional observations
          of my intended prey.

Getting as close as I could,
          I was still wary of a sure shot . . .
raised up, shot, and missed . . . shot again
          as the bird flew away.

Two days later,
          appraised of the event
by a friend, I dispatched my assistant,
          who returned with the bird
in less than an hour.

I immediately began my drawing and
          upon completion, made a
double drawing for the purpose of
          showing all its feathers."

Palm Warbler

**Figure 4. Palm Warbler
(Pl. 163)**

"Subtly patterned brown-and-yellow warblers,
      constantly bobbing tails,
a branch of the wild orange tree . . .
      the rich perfume of the blossoms,
the golden hue of the fruit,
      the deep green of the glossy leaves,
a pleasing effect on the mind . . ."

American Coot

**Figure 5. American Coot
(Pl. 305)**

"Whilst at General Hernandez's in East Florida,
        I found the coot abundant in
every ditch, bayou, and pond.
This was in December 1831,
        and in the next month I saw great flocks
of them near the plantation of
        my friend John Bulow, Esq.

Whilst on a visit to Spring Garden,
        at the head of the St. Johns River,
I observed them to be equally abundant
        along the grassy margins
of the lagoons and lakes.

On my return from the upper parts
        of that river to St. Augustine,
on 28 February,
        I saw large flocks of them
already moving northward.

They had suddenly become shy,
  and would rise before our boat
at a distance of a hundred yards or so,
  with scarcely any apparent difficulty,
and fly in loose flocks at a considerable height,
  half a mile or more at a time,
without uttering a note.

Indeed, the only sound I ever heard
  these birds utter
was a rough guttural note,
  somewhat resembling cruck, cruck,
which they use when alarmed,
  or when chasing each other
on the water in anger."

Audubon in Florida

"Here I am in the Floridas . . .
  which from my childhood
I have consecrated in my imagination
  as the Garden of the United States . . .
Mr. Bartram was the first
  to call this a garden,
but he is to be forgiven:
  he was an enthusiastic botanist,
and rare plants,
  in the eyes of such a man
convert a wilderness
  at once into a garden."

Audubon to Lucy from Florida
Letters, 1831–1832

Audubon,
         You wrote to your wife Lucy,
"My Dearest Friend
         My name is now ranging high and
Our name will stand still higher
         Should I live through
My present travels."

Unlike the earlier Florida traveler
         William Bartram,
you did not find Florida
         a salubrious paradise,
a southern garden.

To Lucy, you declare Florida
         "a wild and dreary and desolate
part of the world . . .
         My account will be
very far from corroborating
         the flowery sayings of Mr. Barton
[Bartram] the botanist."

Audubon,
         You indict St. Augustine as the
"poorest hole in the Creation . . .
         The country around nothing but bare sand
hills . . . hot one day, cold another, etc. etc.
         Sands, poor pine forests, and impenetrable
thickets of cactus and palmettos form the undergrowth."

Audubon,
Why are your Florida images contradictory?
          So different in your letters to Lucy
and your paintings?
          Do you traffic in paradoxes?
Your portrait of a greenshank has
          a sweeping background view:
St. Augustine and
          Castillo de San Marcos in celebrity.

The elusive caracara eagle, which
          you observed flying at a great elevation
near St. Augustine, shot, collected by your assistant, and
          double-drawn by you to show all its
feathers in a classic Picasso manner.

A palm warbler perched on an
          orange tree bough; a Schinz' sandpiper with
sand dunes and ocean tides.
          A herring gull at the entrance to St. Augustine harbor.
All are Florida wilderness images you created,
          Not Bartram.
                    Audubon,
          your huckleberry, persimmon tree, and
wood ibis coursing through canebrake,
          cypress-swamp, and tangled wood;
your discovery of
          Namphaea lutea, the
yellow water lily and
          your plants of the Keys—
Anona, Cyperus (wild poinsettia),
          Convolvululus, Ipomaea and red mangrove
confirm Bartram's Florida garden.
          Audubon,

(continued)

12

you engross Lucy with your premonition:
"I am engaged in an arduous
          undertaking: but if I live to complete it,
I will offer to my country a beautiful monument of the
          varied splendor of American nature, and of my devotion
to American ornithology."

Florida Jay

Figure 6. Florida Jay. East Florida
(Pl. 233)

A non-crested blue jay,
        first noted in Bartram's *Travels*,
was collected and described
        as the Florida jay
during an 1817 expedition
        of the Philadelphia Academy
to Spanish Florida,
        near St. Augustine.

Audubon later observed, painted, and wrote:
        "I have represented a pair
of Florida jays on a branch
        of the persimmon tree,
ornamental with its richly colored fruit."

Wood Ibis

Figure 7. Wood Ibis, South of St. Augustine
(Pl. 316)

"When in St. Augustine,
I was induced to make an excursion
to visit a large pond or lake.
Twenty-three miles,
I trudged through the woods,
and at last came in view of the pond.
When, lo!
Its borders and the trees around
were covered with wood ibises.

The wood ibis takes four years
in attaining full maturity,
although birds of the second year
are now and then found breeding.
This is rare, however, for the young birds
live in flocks by themselves, until
they have attained the age of about three years.

They are at first of a dingy brown,
each feather edged with a paler hue.
The head is covered to the mandibles
with short, downy feathers,
which gradually fall off
as the bird advances in age.
In the third year,
the head is quite bare,
as well as a portion of the upper part
of the neck.
In the fourth year,
the bird is as you see it in the plate.
The male is much larger
and heavier than the female,
but there is no difference
in color between the sexes."

Fish Crow and St. Johns River

**Figure 8. Fish Crow
(Pl. 146 Male and Female)**

"I requested Colonel Rees
 to accompany me in his boat
towards the River St. John,
 as well as to the curious country
in its neighborhood.

As we crossed Rees' Lake,
 I observed that its north-eastern shores
were bounded by a deep swamp
 covered by a rich growth of tall cypresses,
while the opposite side presented
 large marshes and islands
ornamented by pines, live-oaks, and orange.
 And in its waters swam alligators,

(continued)

while ibises, gallinules, anhingas, coots, and cormorants
     were seen pursuing their avocations
on its surface or along its margins.
     Over our heads the fish hawks
sailed,
     and on the broken trees around
we saw many of their nests."

East Florida

Audubon's exploration
     took him south of St. Augustine,   **SEE MAP**
westward, and by land
     to Spring Garden,
and the headwaters
     of the St. Johns.
"Had an island named
     after me —
a complete mass of orange
     trees and live oaks."

His party returned
     by boat and on foot
to St Augustine, and
     then back to Charleston.
From there they would travel
     to the Florida Keys.

3.
To the Florida Keys
    April 19, 1832   **SEE MAP**

On Board the *Marion*

In the beginning of April,
    through the influence
of letters from the Honorable Lewis M'Lean,
    of the Treasury Department,
and the prompt assistance
    of Colonel J. Pringle,
we went on board the revenue cutter the "Marion,"
    commanded by Robert Day, Esq.,
to whose friendly attention
    I am greatly indebted for the success
which I met with in my pursuits,
    during his cruise along the dangerous
coast of East Florida, and amongst the islets
    that every where rise from the surface
of the ocean, like gigantic water-lilies.
    At Indian Key, the Deputy-Collector
afforded me important aid;
    and at Key West I enjoyed
the hospitality of Major Glassel,
    his officers, and their families,
as well as of my friend Dr Benjamin Strobel,
    and other inhabitants of that singular island,
to all of whom I now sincerely offer my best thanks
    for the pleasure which their society afforded me,
and the acquisitions,
    which their ever-ready assistance enabled me to make.

Indian Key
April 25, 1881

As the "Marion" neared the islet
  called "Indian Key,"
on the eastern coast
  of the peninsula of Florida,
my heart swelled with
  uncontrollable delight.
In brief time we stood
  on the desired beach
and gazed on the gorgeous flowers.
  the singular and beautiful plants,
the luxurious trees.
  The birds which we saw
were almost all new to us.
  Their lovely forms appeared
to be arrayed in more brilliant
  apparel than I have
ever seen.

Audubon's Challenge

For many birds
  of the Florida Keys,
the life-size drawings
  for *The Birds of America*
were a size challenge,
  even for an enormous
book,
  more than two feet by three.
Consider the American Flamingo,
  pelicans, egrets and herons.

American Flamingo

"While sailing from Indian Key,
        we spied a flock
of Flamingos
        advancing in "Indian Line,"
with well-spread wings,
        outstretched necks, and
long legs directed backwards.

Ah! Reader, could you know
        the emotions that then
agitated my breast!

I thought I had now reached
        the height of all my
expectations, for my voyage
        to the Floridas."

Brown Pelican

**Figure 10. Brown Pelican
(Pl. 251)**

"The brown pelican,
a constant resident
in the Floridas,
is one of our most
interesting birds.

Standing on their column-like legs,
how dexterously do they wield
that great bill of theirs
as they trim their plumage!
Red mangrove,
represented in the pelican drawing,
is very abundant along the coast
of Florida and on
almost all the Keys.

On arriving
at the Keys of Florida,
I procured many pelican specimens,
but nowhere so many
as at Key West."

Key West

"I was enamored with the Cordia
*   the orange flowering tree*
when I spotted it growing on the property
of my friend, Capt. James Geiger,
*   Key West's first harbor captain.*

I spent months with the Geiger family,
*   sometimes painting on their grounds.*
I named the tree after the family
*   and included its foliage in my drawing*
of two white-crowned pigeons
*   that were among the eighteen*
new species of birds I discovered in Key West."

The Tortugas

**Figure 12. Booby Gannet
(Pl. 426)**

*"As the Marion neared
        the curious islets
of the Tortugas,
        my attention was attracted to
the Booby Gannett.*

*The bills and legs of those in the brown plumage,
        from one to two years of age,
were dusky-blue.*

*These were undergoing moult, and
        at a more advanced age,
the parts mentioned become paler,
        and when the bird has arrived at maturity,
are as represented in my plate.
        I observed no external difference
between the sexes in the adult birds.*

The nearer land we approached,
          the more numerous did they become.
I felt delighted that
          I should have an opportunity
of studying their habits.

I observed ever afterwards
          that they roosted at as
great a height as possible.

Their large flat nests
          they placed on top
of bushes, four to ten feet.
          In all the nests I examined,
only one egg was found.

Back in Key West

Figure 13. Key West Quail-Doves (Key West Pigeons)
(Pl.167)

Audubon and his party
continued their work preparing
specimens and drawings of the area.

To honor the local citizens,
"I have taken it upon myself
to name this species the Key West Pigeon
and offer it as a tribute
to the generous inhabitants of that island,
who favored me with their friendship."

From Key West to Charleston

The *Marion* departed on May 23, 1832,
        with the Audubon party on board.
The next day,
        Dr. Strobel wrote a tribute editorial
in the *Key West Gazette:*
        "Mr. Audubon. This gentleman left here…
for Charleston, calculating to touch
        on his way at the Florida Keys,
and probably the mainland.
        His work on ornithology,
when completed,
        will be the most splendid production
of its kind ever published.
        He is frank, free, and generous,
always willing to impart information
        and to render himself agreeable.
The favorable impressions
        which he has produced upon our minds will not soon be effaced"

In the Upper Keys

Audubon wished to continue
his Florida work during
his trip back to Charleston.

The captain of the *Marion* accommodated
Audubon's wishes by taking detours
before anchoring again at Indian Key.

There, Audubon continued
his earlier work for several days
with visits to Cape Sable and Sandy Key.

He added several birds to his specimens
and drawing portfolios.
Audubon is credited with
the first identification
of the Great White Heron as
a separate species.

"A prize! A prize! A new bird to the American fauna.
Of the fifteen skins
of this species which I carried to Philadelphia,
one was presented to the
Academy of Natural Sciences."

Return to Charleston

Figure 14. Great White Heron, Ardea occidentalis
(Pl. 281)

Audubon returned to Charleston,
     satisfied with his success
in acquiring Florida water birds
     for *The Birds of America* and
his *Ornithological Biography.*
     He contrasted his more ordinary
"land bird" experiences with
     that of *"the water bird,*
which sweeps afar
     over the wide ocean, hovers above the surges,
or betakes itself for refuge
     to the inaccessible rocks
on the shore."
     For the people and the birds, he noted
"Seldom have I experienced greater pleasure
     than on the Florida Keys."

Epilogue

In Philadelphia

Back in Philadelphia, Audubon wrote: *"The natives are quite astonished at my production and collections, etc. G. Ord has caused a most violent attack on my veracity to be issued in a London Journal; how he will stand mine eye on Tuesday next at the Society is more than I can at present tell."* At the Academy meeting on July 17, 1832, the minutes noted with appreciation that Audubon had already presented the Academy with the first volume of his *Ornithological Biography*. The minutes also record that *"Dr. [Charles] Pickering remarked of the birds presented this evening that they are part of a large collection made by Mr. Audubon in Florida, that several are now added to the catalogue of species of the United States."*

Audubon had hoped to continue his quest for birds in Florida in 1833 with his son, John. However, the pressures of completing *The Birds of America and Ornithological Biography* would delay their plans until 1837. On February 17 of that year, Audubon departed overland in and around Pensacola from Charleston with his son and Edward Harris for several days. They would go on to New Orleans and the western Gulf coast, returning overland in mid-May from Mobile to Charleston.

Audubon published the second volume of *Ornithological Biography* in 1834, the third in 1835, the fourth in 1838, and the final volume in 1839. He completed *The Birds of America* folios in 1838. Subsequently, Audubon and his sons published combined editions of the two works using conventional sized plates for the illustrations.

Audubon's Botanicals

Should you
      good-natured reader
be a botanist
      I hope you will find
pleasure
      while looking at
the flowers, the herbs,
      the shrubs, and the trees that
I have represented;
      the more so, I imagine,
if you have seen them
      in their native woods.

Audubon's "Great Work"

The Birds of America
>made him famous.
A tremendous artistic
>and ornithological achievement.
A massive four-volume compendium
>of avian art.
Four-hundred thirty-five engraved images
>of some four-hundred ninety bird species.
Impressive in scale,
>each bird depicted in the "size of life."
Bird images as real
>as reality itself, for
the viewer to study each bird
>closer and longer than
ever possible in the field.
>Stunning visual impact.
Ambitious in its reach.
>A product of personal passion
and sacrifice.

Postscripts

It is standard procedure to list works consulted when writing about the past, even in fiction or poetry. For an individual like John James Audubon, for whom published self-writings are legion, these references include books, articles, and letters, along with many biographies and legends. An avid reader I have been for a lifetime, and the writer of "With Audubon," Chapter 8 of *Florida Explored: The Philadelphia Connection in Bartram's Tracks.* Audubon recorded his observations and data in his extensive daily writings and drawings. These were the basis for his *Journals, Ornithological Biography, Episodes,* and *The Birds of America.* These became the primary references for the poems in this anthology. For the reader, **Poem** References are a guide for Audubon quotes or paraphrasing. **General References** is the more extensive list. **Figures** lists the label and plate reference.

General References

Arthur, Stanley Clisby. *Audubon: An Intimate Life of the American Woodsman*. (Gretna, LA: Pelican Publishing Company, 2000).

Audubon, John James. *The Birds of America from Original Drawings*. [Sometimes called the Havell Edition after its printer, and sometimes called the "Double Elephant Folio" because of its size, it was printed on handmade paper 39.5 inches tall by 28.5 inches wide. The work consists of 435 hand-colored, life-size prints. Other sized editions were later published, up to the present, including online versions.] 4 volumes privately published by Audubon, London, 1827–1838.]

Audubon, John James. *Letters of John James Audubon, 1826–1840*. Edited by Henry Corning, volumes 1–2. (Boston, MA: The Club of Odd Volumes, 1930).

Audubon, John James. *John James Audubon: Writings and Drawings*. Edited by Christoph Irmscher. (New York, NY: Literary Classics of the United States, 1999), 159–92.

Audubon, John James. *Ornithological Biography*, or *An Account of the Habits of the Birds of the United States of America*. (Edinburgh, UK: Neill & Co. for Adam & Charles Black and R. Havell Jun. and Longman, Rees, Brown and Green (London), and various others, Edinburgh & London, 1835; Andesite Press, 2017). [Accompanied by descriptions of the objects represented in the work entitled *The Birds of America* and interspersed with delineations of American scenery and manners. Online versions.]

Audubon, John James. *Synopsis of the Birds of North America.* (London, UK: Longman, Rees, Brown, Green, and Longman, 1839).

Audubon, Maria R. *Audubon and His Journals*, volumes 1–2. (New York, NY: Dover Publications Inc., 1994). [Reprint of 1897 edition.]

Bartram, William. *Travels, or Travels Through North and South Carolina, Georgia, East and West Florida, The Cherokee Country, The Extensive Territories of the Muscogules, or Creek Confederacy, and the Country of the Choctaws: Containing an Account of the Soil and Natural Productions of those Regions, Together with Observations on the Manners of the Indians* (Philadelphia, PA: James and Johnston, 1791).

Ford, Alice. *John James Audubon: A Biography.* (New York, NY: Abbeville Press, 1988).

Ford, Alice. *The 1826 Journal of John James Audubon.* (Norman, OK: University of Oklahoma Press, 1967).

Herrick, Francis Hobart. *Audubon the Naturalist: A History of his Life and Time*, Volume 2. (New York, NY: Dover, 1968).

Peck, Robert McCracken and Patricia Tyson Stroud. *A Glorious Enterprise: The Academy of Natural Sciences of Philadelphia and the Making of American Science.* (Philadelphia, PA: University of Pennsylvania Press, 2012).

Proby, Kathryn Hall. *Audubon in Florida.* (Coral Gables, FL: University of Miami Press, 1974).

Rhodes, Richard. *John James Audubon: The Making of an American.* (New York, NY: Knopf, Borzoi Books, 2004).

Rhodes, Richard. *The Audubon Reader.* (New York: Everyman's
    Library, Knopf, 2006).

Streshinsky, Shirley. *Audubon Life and Art in the American
    Wilderness.* (New York, NY: Villard, 1993).

Welker, Robert Henry. *Birds and Men: American Birds in Sciences,
    Art, Literature, and Conservation, 1800–1900.* (New York, NY:
    Atheneum, 1966).

Poem References
"Audubon quotes or paraphrasing, drawings, and plates."

A Dream, Bennett, *Goose River Anthology, 2022*
       (Waldoboro, ME. **Goose River Press, 2022).**

Charleston, Herrick, Vol. 2.

At Charleston, Corning, Vol. 1.

Charleston to St. Augustine, Corning, Vol. 1.

St. Augustine in November, Corning, Vol. 1.

Caracara Eagle, *Ornithological Biography*, Vol. 2.

Palm Warbler, *Ornithological Biography*, Vol. 2.

American Coot, *Ornithological Biography*, Vol. 2.

Audubon in Florida, Bennett, *Goose River Anthology, 2022.*

Audubon to Lucy from Florida, Corning, Vol. 1.

Florida Jay, *Ornithological Biography*, Vol. 2.

Wood Ibis, *Ornithological Biography*, Vol. 3.

Fish Crow and St. Johns River, *Ornithological Biography*, Vol. 2.

East Florida, *Ornithological Biography*, Vol. 2.

On Board the Marion, *Ornithological Biography*, Vol. 2.

Indian Key, *Ornithological Biography*, Vol. 2.

Audubon's Challenge

American Flamingo, *Ornithological Biography*, Vol. 5.

Brown Pelican, *Ornithological Biography*, Vol. 3.

Key West, *Ornithological Biography*, Vol. 2.

The Tortugas, *Ornithological Biography*, Vol. 3.

Back in Key West, *Ornithological Biography*, Vol. 2.

From Key West to Charleston

In the Upper Keys, *Ornithological Biography*, Vol. 3.

Return to Charleston

Figures

"PL refers to plate number in Audubon's Bird of America."

Map of Audubon's Florida Travels
Figure 1. Long-billed Curlews (Pl. 346)
Figure 2. Greenshank. St. Augustine (Pl.231)
Figure 3. Caracara. Near St. Augustine (Pl. 161)
Figure 4. Palm Warbler (Pl.163)
Figure 5. American Coot (Pl.305)
Figure 6. Florida Jay (Pl.233)
Figure 7 Wood Ibis (Pl.316)
Figure 8. Fish Crow (Pl.146)
Figure 9. American Flamingo (Pl. 431)
Figure 10. Brown Pelican (Pl.251)
Figure 11. White-Crowned Pigeon and Geiger Tree (Pl. 177)
Figure 12. Booby Gannet (Pl. 426)
Figure 13. Key West Quail-Doves (Key West Pigeons) (Pl.167)
Figure 14. Great White Heron, *Ardea occidentalis* (Pl. 281)

About the Author

Thomas Peter Bennett is a Florida native on perpetual sabbatical as an independent scholar and poet. A former professor and natural history museum executive, he has published scientific articles and books, as well as poems and collections on topics featured in *John Audubon Explores Florida: Poems*. This book is largely drawn from Bennett's research and field explorations in the "new U.S. Territory, FLORIDA."

A graduate of Florida State University (FSU), Bennett earned his Ph.D. in biochemistry from the Rockefeller University and became an assistant professor at Harvard University. He later returned to FSU as a professor and the chair of biological sciences, afterwards serving as the special assistant to the president and acting executive vice president. His museum work began with his appointment as the president of the Academy of Natural Sciences of Philadelphia, now the Academy of Natural Sciences of Drexel University. After a decade at the Academy, he returned to Florida as a dean, professor, and the director of the Florida Museum of Natural History at the University of Florida. Ten years later, he became the executive director of the South Florida Museum and retired as an emeritus executive director.

While teaching at FSU, Bennett started publishing poetry, attended workshops with Michael Bugeja and others, and studied with Mary Oliver at Bennington College. Bennett's recent poems—inspired by the natural wonders in Florida and Maine—have appeared in *Red Owl, Chebacco, POETALK, The Café Review, Puckerbrush Review, Pegasus Review,* and *Perspectives in Biology and Medicine,* among others, and in various anthologies, such as *Goose River Anthology, Cosmos Club Poets Through the Years,* and *Bay Area Poets Coalition.* He is the author of several poetry chapbooks and seven books of poetry including: *Nature, As One Sees It* (2003), *A Celebration of John and William Bartram: In Philadelphia and Florida* (2005), *Hike On* (2008), *Encore Seasons* (2017), *Florida* Sketches (2019), and *The Applause of Science* (2021).

In addition to his poetry and scientific works, Bennett has several textbooks and historical scientific books to his credit: *The Legacy: South Florida Museum* (2010), *The Le Contes: Scientific Family of Woodmanston* (2014), and *Florida Explored: The Philadelphia Connection in Bartram's Tracks* (2019). He is a member of The Explorers Club and the Cosmos Club.